Little healers: Chakras

Written by Becky Payne
Illustrated by Romina Petra

To my twin sister Sarah.

Thank you for all of your support as we walk through life together.

I wouldn't be who I am without you.

Chakras are beautiful wheels of energy in your body.

You have seven chakras or energy centers.

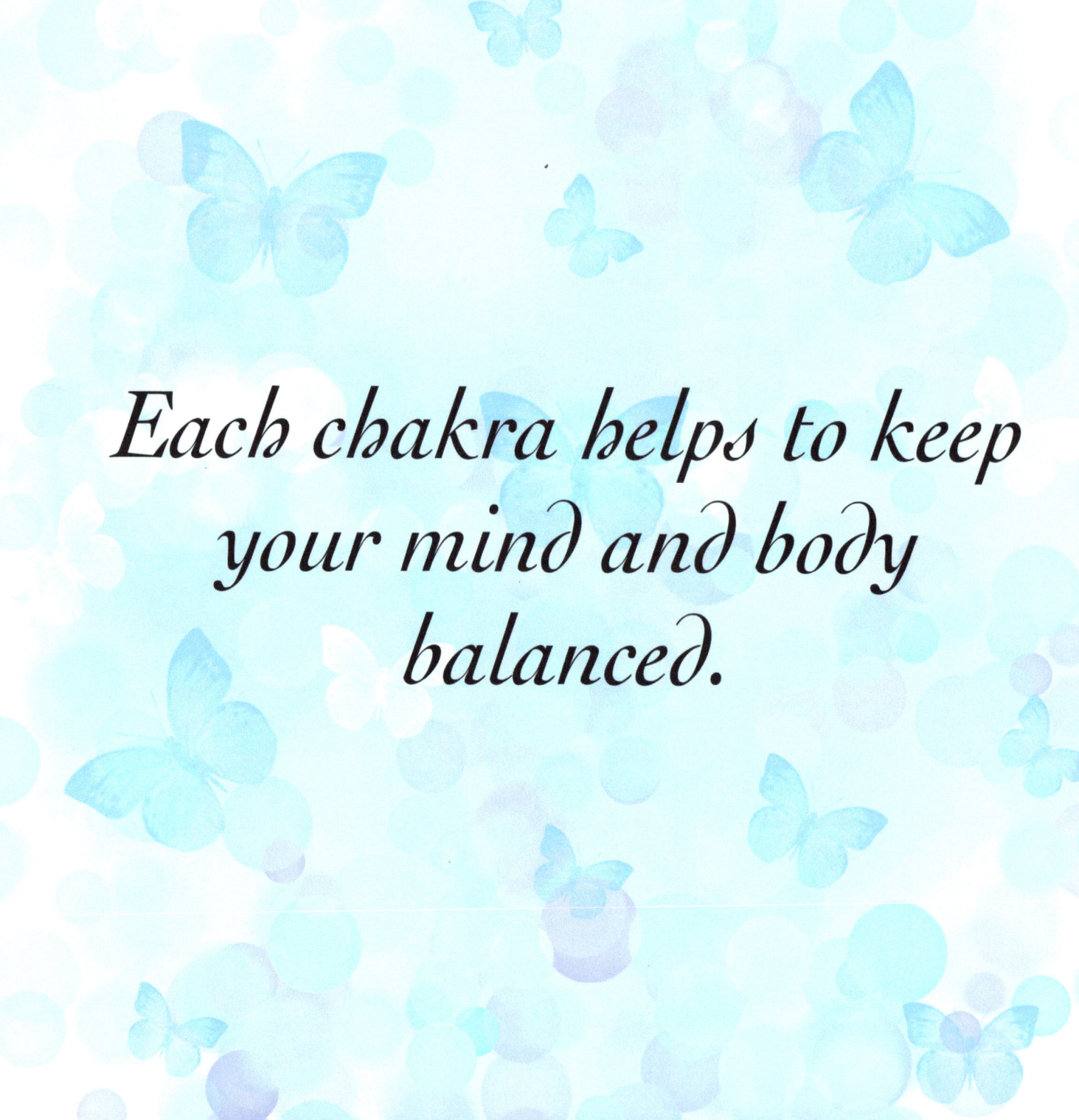

Each chakra helps to keep your mind and body balanced.

You can help keep your chakras balanced by repeating an affirmation for each chakra. Let's get started!

Root chakra is red. It keeps you safe and grounded. Say, "I am grounded".

Sacral chakra is orange. It gives you creative energy. Say, "I am creative".

Solar plexus chakra is yellow. It helps you stay confident. Say, "I am confident".

Heart chakra is green. It is your center of love and compassion. Say, "I love myself".

Throat chakra is blue. It helps you communicate. Say, "I speak clearly".

Third eye chakra is indigo. It gives you intuition. Say, "I trust myself".

Crown chakra is purple. It is your connection to other people and to the world. Say, "I am connected".

Help keep your chakras balanced by repeating each affirmation. Be well Little Healer!

www.ingramcontent.com/pod-product-compliance
Lightning Source LLC
Chambersburg PA
CBHW041714160426
43209CB00018B/1835